Introduction

Newbridge on Wye is a village of some ⟨…⟩ the junction of two ancient routes, one whic⟨…⟩ the other which followed the Wye valley north ⟨…⟩ led, picturesque hollow of the Wye River vall⟨…⟩ the Cambrian Mountains to the west with the Eppynt Hills and Carneddau to the south. Unusually for a Radnorshire village it has a central village green as a nucleus from which the houses and roads radiate out. Although most of the stone built houses pre-date the 20th Century and a few, like the New Inn, reach back several hundred years, quite a lot of development has taken place in the post-war years with about a hundred houses being added in the 1980's and more such as the Riverside estate in the 1990's and into the new millennium. Today the village has several shops, a post office, a primary school and two public houses. Community spirit is still evident with a range of organisations and activity groups from Fishing and Football to the W.I. For many years there has been an agricultural show, a carnival, a sheep dog trial, an eisteddfod and trotting races all set in this magnificent mid-Wales countryside.

This booklet describes the history of Newbridge and its surroundings by reference to the village's bridges, church, school, railway and people. Together they provide a fascinating view of the village over the last two centuries and the social and environmental change which has taken place.

The history of the area can be traced from Iron Age hill forts and Roman baths through a thousand years of church history to the mechanised and industrial bustle of the 21st Century – however, in Newbridge quiet corners of natural interest still remain.

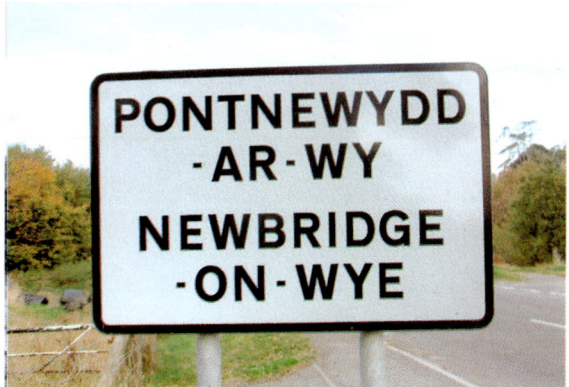

PONTNEWYDD -AR-WY NEWBRIDGE -ON-WYE

We invite you to join us on a journey through an unforgettable area of Wales....

Rhagarweiniad

Mae Pontnewydd ar Wy yn bentref gyda poblogaeth o ryw 500 o fobl. Mae wedi ei ddatblygu ar gyffordd dau hen lwybr, un sydd yn croesi'r afon gorllewin-dwyrain a'r un arall yn dilyn dyffryn yr Wy o'r gogledd i'r de. Mae'r pentref yn gorwedd mewn man cysgodol, darluniaidd o dyffryn Afon Wy, i'r gorllewin mae godrefryniau Mynyddoedd Cambria a Bryniau Epynt a'r Carneddau i'r dde. Yn anghyffredin i bentref Maesyfed mae'r tai a'r ffyrdd yn pelydru allan o lawnt canolig sydd fel cnewyllyn i Bontnewydd. Er bod y rhan fwyaf o'r adeiladau cerrig wedi'u hadeiladu cyn yr ugeinfed ganrif, a rhai, fel Tafarn Newydd gyda hanes nifer o ganrifoedd yn ôl, mae llawer o'r datblygiadau wedi bod yn y blynyddoedd ôl- rhyfel gyda rhyw gant o adeiladau wedi ychwanegu yn y 1980au a llawer mwy ers stadau Riverside yn y 1990au ac i fewn i'r mileniwm. Heddiw mae yn y pentref nifer o siopau, siop y post, ysgol gynradd a dau dafarn. Mae ysbryd gymunedol yn dal i fodoli gyda amrediad o fudiadau a grwpiau gweithredol o Bysgota a Pêl-droed i Sefydliad y Merched. Am llawer o flynyddoedd mae sioe amaethyddol wedi cael ei chynnal, carnifal, treialon cwn defaid, eisteddfod a rasus trottio, i gyd yn cael ei cynnal yng nghefri gwlad hardd Canolbarth Cymru.

Mae'r llyfryn yma yn disgirfio hanes Bontnewydd a'i amgylchedd gyda cyfeiriadau i bontydd y pentref, yr eglwys, ysgol, rheilffordd a'r pobl. Gyda'i gilydd maent yn darparu golygfa bendigedig o'r pentref dros y ddwy ganrif olaf, yn ogystal yn edrych ar y newidiadau cymdeithasol ac amgylcheddol sydd wedi digwydd. Er bod hanes yr ardal yn gallu cael ei olrheinio o'r Oes Haearn â bryn fel caer, y baddon Rhufeiniaid drwy mil o flynyddoedd o hanes eglwys, ac i fywyd mecanyddol ac diwydiannol yr ugeinfed ganrif.

Heddiw, yn Bontnewydd mae corneli o ddiddordebau natur yn dal i fodoli.

Rydym yn eich croesawu chi i ymuno â ni ar siwrnau drwy rhan bythgofiadwy o Gymru....

History

Although the village of Newbridge probably grew following the construction of the first bridge there has, since time immemorial, been a crossing point for the river in this vicinity. There is an **ancient standing stone** (pictured right) of unknown age in the riverside field near Penbont Farm. Such stones are thought to be ancient way markers and there can be no doubt that this was a crossing place from the earliest times as a bridge of this span would only have been placed where it is because of roads or tracks leading to it.

People first colonised the area during the **Neolithic** or **"New Stone Age"** around 4000 BC. Pollen data show that a comparatively sharp decline in elm at around this time may have been caused by clearance of forests to make room for cultivated crops and use of elm foliage as fodder for cattle.

Bronze Age people lived in the Wye valley from around 2000 BC onwards, possibly using the river itself as a route inland. Remains of this period have been found as near as Llysdinam, Llanwrthwl, Nantmel, in the form of cairns – the most important concentration of such in Wales is in the Elan Valley uplands. These people also used hilltop ridgeways such as the Kerry Ridgeway as long distance routes. It is possible that the old lane – shown as such by the age of its hedges – which runs behind Llysdinam House and can be traced back to the river near the present picnic site at Llyn Cam, could be access to an ancient east west trackway.

The **Romans** conquered Wales by around 78 AD and evidence of their occupation can be seen at several locations in Radnorshire, most notably at **Castell Collen** in Llanyre parish which seems to have been a major fort (see page 48). It was established originally around 73-78 AD and is one of the very few forts to show unmistakable evidence of occupation after 170 AD.

The **Romans** usually crossed the Wye nearer Builth Road but when the Ithon was in spate it is probable that they, like many before and since, crossed the river at Newbridge. Travellers in other directions would also have used the Newbridge ford. A 14th Century map of South Wales indicates a road or track at right angles to the Roman route, from NW to SE almost certainly crossing the Wye at the Newbridge ford.

There is little evidence of what happened in this area during the "𝕯𝖆𝖗𝖐 𝕬𝖌𝖊𝖘" that followed the retreat of the Roman troops from Britain in 410. After the 𝕹𝖔𝖗𝖒𝖆𝖓 𝕮𝖔𝖓𝖖𝖚𝖊𝖘𝖙 of Britain in 1066 Norman settlers spread through England and Wales. The de Braose family became dominant in Elfael in the south of what would become Radnorshire whilst the Mortimers conquered Maelenydd (in the east) and Gwyrthrynion (in the west). In 1292 Edward Mortimer was granted the right by Edward I to hold a weekly market and 2 annual fairs in Newbridge parish but they were short lived and there was no mention of them by 1304, presumably because established markets and fairs like those held at Builth and Rhayader made them superfluous.

The County of Radnorshire in which Newbridge lies dates from 1536 when it was created under Henry VIII's "𝕬𝖈𝖙 𝖔𝖋 𝖀𝖓𝖎𝖔𝖓" and came under the laws of the rest of England and Wales for the first time. The Medieval name for the region was "Rhwng Gwy a Hafren" meaning the land "between the Wye and the Severn".

3

There is little information to show when the bridge over the Wye was first built. The farm on the Breconshire side of the crossing is called Penbont (bont=bridge) but there is no evidence of a former Welsh name for Newbridge. Leland in his itinerary written in 1543 after mentioning the Wye Bridge at Builth says, "There is no other bridge on the Wye from Hereford to Builth, upwards there is a bridge newly repaired of timber.". A map by Saxton dated 1610 clearly shows bridges at Rhayader, Newbridge, Builth and Glasbury. "The bridge upwards from Builth" may mean Newbridge or Rhayader. It is therefore possible that the bridge existed as far back as 1543 and was in need of repair by that date.

There is little further mention of the area until the 16th Century, when, in some papers dated 1587, the then considerable sum of £320 was being asked for the possession of Woodcastle Farm, which lies on the south eastern fringe of the village. There is said to be reference in Welsh History to fighting having taken place at some time near Woodcastle, and across the Ithon to the south of it at Bwlch Bryn in the Parish of Disserth. There is some evidence of a defensive structure here although it does not appear to hold a strong defensive position. Mr D. Davies, whose family lived at Woodcastle for three generations said that when his family first moved there, the door from the "castle" was still in use on the stable: it was massive and heavy and thickly studded with large headed iron nails. He added that the site of the castle had been the flat piece below the house and indeed there are signs that a former building existed at that

Woodcastle Farmland Today

location until the 19th Century. Woodcastle controlled all the enclosed land from Disserth to the Wye confluence and then up the Wye to Aberithon.

The Church in Wales

The history of the Church in Wales has, to say the least, been turbulent. In pre-Tudor times the church was essentially Catholic but the purge of Cromwell's times removed almost all church items which were associated with Catholicism. The publication in 1588 of William Morgan's Welsh translation of the Bible and the appearance in mid-Wales of some leading itinerant Puritan preachers such as Walter Cradock and Vavasor Powell lead to a revival of religious interest. Powell, a Radnorshire man born in Knucklas in 1617, became a Baptist and helped to strengthen the county as one of the first strongholds of Baptists in the Principality.

The original Pentref Baptist Chapel built in 1759 (right).

The "new" Pentref Baptist Chapel, built in 1879 (below).

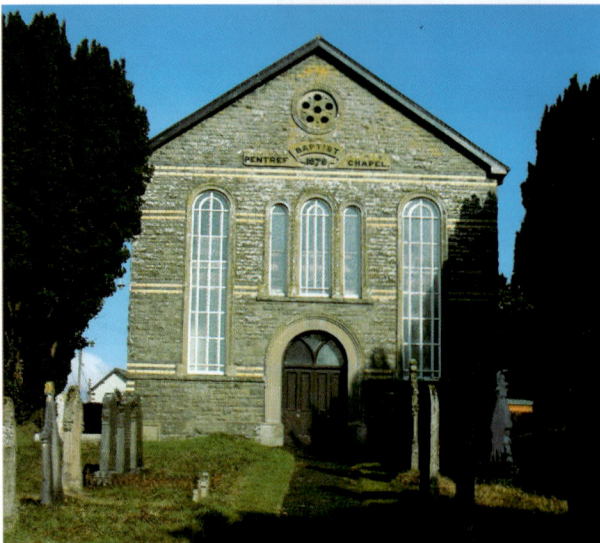

A small Wesleyan chapel was, until 1950, also active in the village. It was, however, in 1958 converted into a private house.

The Drovers

Droving began in the late 17th Century because the growing English towns and cities, particularly London, found it difficult to feed themselves from local sources only, as they had in the past. Wales and Scotland were willing and able to supply what was needed. The uplands of Wales and Scotland excelled in livestock production but England provided rich grazing grounds for fattening and the fairs and markets at which the animals could finally be sold. This trade became Wales' overwhelmingly most important export until the Industrial development in South Wales.

A present day photograph of "The Monk's Trod" (right) – an ancient Drovers route which passes over the Cambrian Mountains from Strata Florida to Abbeycwmhir north east of Rhayader.

Newbridge lies along one of the most famous Welsh drove routes which begins at Tregaron and runs across the wide moorland to Abergwesyn and continues on to Beulah, where it then, more or less, follows the B4358 to Newbridge passing the Red Lion at Llanafan Fawr along the way. From Newbridge one route passes Woodcastle Farm and heads east via Disserth, Howey, Glascwm and Gladestry and then over the border to Kington. The Welsh head-drover was usually entrusted with the livestock by the farmer, paying for them on his return from the markets and fairs of England.

A man could only apply for a droving licence if he was over thirty, married and a householder. Any man driving cattle without a licence faced a fine. Drovers were forbidden from working on the Sabbath and could again incur a financial penalty for doing so.

The drovers played a vital part in the forging of an economic and cultural link between England and Wales which was of benefit to both countries. Money in cash was carried as little as possible and this became an important factor in the development of modern banking with the use of bills of exchange as an alternative to cash due to the danger of being robbed along the way.

A banknote issued by David Jones's bank at Llandovery

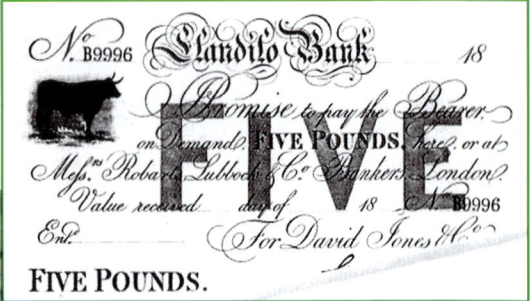

Welsh Black cattle (left) – the breed usually herded by the drovers.

In the 18th Century, Drovers' routes with turnpike tolls at each tollgate made a great difference to a drover's profits and were avoided, if necessary by extra mileage, which is why many of the drovers routes go over hilltops and through remote, hazardous areas.

The animals on the droves had to be shod to travel along metalled roads and there were many blacksmith's forges along the main drovers routes. The shoes, called *Ciws* in Wales, were lighter than horse shoes and adapted for cloven hooves so eight were required per beast. Geese were driven through a mixture of pitch and sand which hardened and formed a protective barrier on their feet. Pigs were given "boots" – little woollen socks with leather soles.

In order to make their journey successfully, Drovers needed refreshment and overnight accommodation for themselves and their livestock. The "inns" were often simply farms which made a surplus of their own brew to sell to travellers. Even now many Welsh pubs share their building with a farm. A local example is the Red Lion at Llanafan, said to be possibly the oldest pub in Wales. In addition to beer, cider became popular in Wales in the 18th Century and cider houses became common along many of the drovers routes. In the open country a farmer who wanted to let drovers know that he was able to provide food, accommodation and grazing did so by planting three Scots pines outside his farmhouse.

Entertainment was provided at many of the inns when the drovers were there, fiddlers came and there was dancing, singing and sometimes boxing and wrestling. This carousing could be very lively and Newbridge was no exception with no less than thirteen public houses at one time and a house, now called Merry Hall, was once known as Merry Hell!

The droving way of life existed for about 300 years before being replaced by railways which provided a quicker more efficient way of transporting livestock.

A statue of a solitary drover has been put up on the village green in Newbridge-on-Wye to represent the strong historical link between the Drovers and the development of the village.

19th Century Newbridge

In the 19th Century the variety of crops grown was wider than it is today. In addition to wheat, oats and potatoes, hops were grown certainly as far back as Roman times and flax was produced for linen from at least Tudor times. This trade carried on in parts of Radnorshire certainly into the 19th Century when flax was grown, woven and made into linen smocks, particularly in the north east of the county. Until well into the 20th Century the clog trade of northern England received much of its supply of Alder wood for soles from itinerant woodmen coppicing the alder woods of the Wye Valley. The corn produced on local farms was milled by water mills. There was an "Old Mill" recorded near the Dyfnant brook in the village, but they were also to be found at Howey, Disserth, Cwmbach, Doldowlod, Llanwrthwl and on several streams on the road to Beulah.

At this time there were about 30 houses in the village, many of which still stand. Fuel for these houses would have been from the turbaries (peat bogs), Aberithon to the south and Vedw to the north of the village and a further turbary on the hills north of the village near the present day television transmitter.

Prior to the Enclosure Acts of the 1840's over one third of the land in the parish was unenclosed with much of the periphery of the village being common land, including Rostrow Common to the north, Aberithon to the south plus Old Mill Common along what is now Cyffredin Lane. The Acts meant that many villagers lost their homes and livelihoods as the common land was sold, fenced off and absorbed into the great estates.

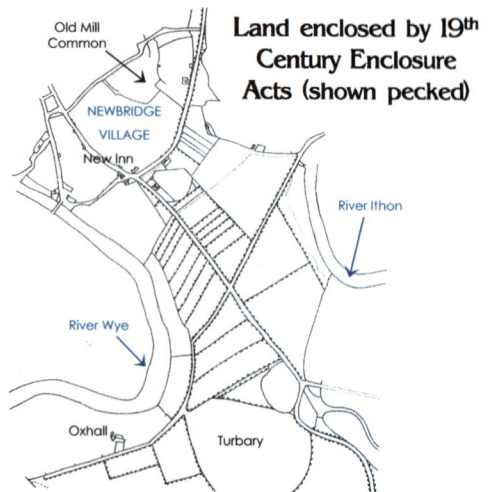

Land enclosed by 19th Century Enclosure Acts (shown pecked)

The land that had been used for grazing the sheep and cows that provided people with their only form of sustenance was gone, now their only possibility of work was to become a servant of such an estate. The remainder became tradesmen and artisans who served the needs of the village such as drapers, ironmongers, farm suppliers, butchers, grocers, shoemakers, and blacksmiths.

A 19th Century Blacksmith at work.

Newbridge, together with Rhayader, St Harmon, Howey and areas of South Wales gained some notoriety in the period 1843-4 when the so-called Rebecca Riots took place. The rioters blackened their faces and wore women's dress as a disguise when they attacked turnpike gates as protests against unfair tolls on farm produce. They also attacked unpopular magistrates and clergy and returned illegitimate children, who had been put out to nurse, to the homes of their wealthy fathers.

In protest against the Fishery Laws, salmon poachers adopted the same name and disguise and took to the rivers during the second half of the 19th Century. As late as 1904, in Rhayader, navvies building the Elan Valley dams took part and 200 salmon, some weighing 30-40 lbs were taken on a single occasion. After a similar event in 1907 salmon in Rhayader fetched 3d (just over 1p) per pound. The Sun Inn in Newbridge, demolished in the mid 1970's was at one time locally referred to as a Rebecca House.

The village's first postmaster was introduced in 1848 and the Post Office employed a postman who sorted and delivered the mail on foot, even on Sundays!

Newbridge became part of the country's new railway system, in part due to the influence of two local families, the Venables and the Gibson-Watts. Archdeacon Venables of Llysdinam Hall had been a Director of the Gloucester-Aberystwyth Central Wales Railway and possessed a network of important aristocratic connections. The Gibson Watt family of Doldowlod's illustrious ancestor, James Watt, had greatly contributed to the railway's development by his part in the development of the steam engine.

Newbridge-on-Wye Station

Train entering Newbridge-on-Wye Station

In 1862, the mid-Wales Line connected Newbridge with Brecon to the south and, by changing, Aberystwyth to the north, traversing with its tracks some of the most spectacularly beautiful countryside to be seen in the British Isles.

The addition of the railway totally altered the lives of the villagers; it provided jobs such as porters and platelayers and easier means of travel allowing the men to seek jobs elsewhere, such as in the mines and iron works of South Wales. It also provided transport for ready-made goods and building materials and meant that coal could be brought in by train, replacing the need for peat turbaries.

Newbridge a generation or two ago...

By the mid 19th Century, the population of the village was about 700 and like most of Radnorshire little Welsh was spoken. Some villagers had lived in Newbridge for generations but the remainder were transient and stayed for only a few months, usually arriving in May when jobs were sought and bestowed at the annual Hiring Fair. This was the time of year when servants and farm labourers changed their jobs and the Hiring Fair served as the primary source for employment for the area until the 1930's.

The hiring fair took place on the first Friday after 13th May and allowed farmers to hire servants for the next 12 months. Hiring fairs were also held at the same time of year at nearby Builth Wells and at Rhayader. At the fair, it was customary for the young men seeking jobs to wear smocks or slop jackets and for the ladies to wear check aprons. Once the individual had been hired the jackets and aprons were removed. A Newbridge resident recalled, "The job seekers would stand around and wait for the farmers to go up and talk to them about employment and terms. There was the question of 'earnest money' which bound the agreement and, if broken, would have to be returned to the farmer in question.". Most workers were hired for a year at a time, although some farm servants were hired for only six months until October, covering the most productive period of the farming year.

Hiring servants in this way rapidly declined at the turn of the 20th Century when May (and a Mr Marshall Evans) brought the new Pleasure Fair to Newbridge, usually on the 16th, with swingboats, hoopla, coconut shies, skittles, shooting galleries plus gingerbread and fruit stalls.

There were also two Horse Fairs held annually on 19th October and 11th November. The former was called the Great Horse Fair. By 5am the horses were passing the Bell Inn at Llanyre and the "road fairing" people, who followed fairs from place to place, would be leaving the village field at Llanyre where they had been camping (and not infrequently fighting) for several days prior to the fair. The horses arrived in the village between 7 and 8 o'clock in the morning and were lined up from Woodland Cottages in the south, to beyond the Beulah turn in the north, under the (still existing) railway arch and down towards the river Wye ford and again back up the Llandrindod road. The railway worked overtime bringing trucks full of cobs, hill ponies and shires, and transporting them again after the sales although some of the old drovers still preferred to bring them by road, four or five tied head to tail. Prior to the Licensing Act of 1872 there would have been long lines of drinking booths but such laws did not stop the conviviality of the occasion.

The day ended with many local inhabitants standing near the station to watch the horses being loaded onto wagons.

These scenes were repeated annually until after the Second World War when mechanisation replaced the horse.

Other than at the Autumn fairs, stock was regularly sold at the small livestock markets in March, July, September and at Christmas when cattle, sheep and pigs came under the hammer. In the early 20th Century the market was held in the field behind the post office, and later, on the northern boundary of the village opposite the B4558 turn for Beulah where the prisoner of war camp was built during the Second World War.

13

Subsequently in the late 1930's the market moved to a permanent mart-yard adjacent to the New Inn where it finally closed in 1959. The pen marks can still be seen today in the upper section of the New Inn Car park. Village children benefited from the cattle trade. As cattle markets were held in Rhayader every Wednesday, buyers from farms south of Newbridge-on-Wye would have to drive their cattle through the village. En route the farmers would engage the local children to drive their cattle approximately half a mile south whilst they enjoyed a meal at the Golden Lion or the New Inn. The Golden Lion was renowned far and wide for serving an excellent meal for 2 shillings and 6 pence. This meal was locally known as the "Goose Dinner." Whilst they were enjoying their meal their animals, in the charge of the children, would be guided along the road avoiding many open lanes. The farmer, suitably refreshed would then catch up with the children and pay them 1 penny for their troubles.

The Annual Foresters' Fete was held around the third Friday in June every year. The Foresters Club was a Friendly Society to which members paid an annual fee. It's motto was, "the Bow of Benevolence... Speeding the Arrow of Assistance," and the Club provided people with financial assistance in the event of illness or injury, and also some death benefits. This assistance was of great help in the days before the creation of the National Health Service. The Fete comprised a large, well-attended procession of riders, all wearing hats and dressed in green trousers and red stockings, with tunics made of laurel leaves, led by a rider clothed as Robin Hood, and one lady rider. It was a day long event held annually and the tradition lasted well into the 20th Century.

Not every day was as easy as a fair day, for perhaps tomorrow the farmer would be transporting 250 lb sacks of grain four or five at a time on the chassis of a cart, (the cart itself being removed to save weight) to the mill at Cwmbach on the road to Builth. In the 19th Century the reaping of the corn would have been done with a sickle and it would take seven or eight men to reap three acres of grain a day. In addition to the corn harvest, autumn was also the time when the travelling cider press would come through the village to help turn surplus apples into a potent brew.

Because of its importance as a meeting, place there were at one time 13 public houses in the village. So many indeed that Cara Venables (sister to Lady Katherine Minna Venables of Llysdinam Hall) bought The Oak to do away with its licence.

In October 1926 George Jones began a daily bus service to Llandrindod and a service to Builth Wells market on Monday. He was also the owner of a haulage business and the two garages in the village.

There were two banks in the village, the London City & Midland at Cartref, close to the railway arch and the Midland Bank opened on Fair days at a house called Mellindwr.

A well known character in the village between the wars was "Harry Clocky", an excellent watch maker and repairer. He went around the farms repairing clocks and he expected to be offered tea by his customers more or less as soon as he had arrived. On one occasion, the story is told, he called at a farm to repair their clock and no tea arrived, so he put the clock back together again so that it worked backwards and then left. He was half way down the field when he heard the farmers wife screaming after him that her clock was going backwards and Harry Clocky replied "yes, that's the way my tea went.". When radio and television came out he spent most of his time making radios (he even made his own coils), he then had very little time for clocks and watches. He would tune into America very early every morning and people would call in and listen with him. He was just one of the many people in the village running shops and small businesses in pre or early post-war Newbridge.

In the early part of the 20th Century, Newbridge was a thriving village with a virtually self-sufficient economy. Next door to Glanant was the saddlers shed, and near the Mid Wales pub (now a private house) was Thomas's Boot Shop where boots and shoes were made and repaired with the aid of two cobblers. The shoe wax supplied by the shop was homemade. There was also a second Shoe shop in the village.

There were two bakeries, one near the church at The Dot and the other still working until the 1990's, the Cambrian Steam Bakery adjoining the former Alfords Shop (right).

Here their first delivery vehicle was a pony and trap but later they used a Ford van registration No: FO 585 (left).

In between the wars there were also grocers at the Lion shop, Hopes (now a private house) and Mellindwr as well as a small shop in Crown Row. Next to the village green on the Llandrindod road was a fish and chip shop. Two butchers shops, one in Crown row and one at Lower House plus three slaughter houses to which can be added two blacksmiths, a builder, a monumental mason,

Hopes Stores - 1917

two drapers and tailors (one of which employed four full time tailors), a china shop, a Post Office (which moved from Upper Shop – now Skylarks near the New Inn – to Brooklyn, and eventually to its present site), a brew house, shops selling coal and paraffin or cattle feed and meal.

Newbridge looking South – 1904.

The road to Rhayader, looking North – 1917

Prior to the coming of the railway, domestic fuel was often peat cut from one of the village turbaries. Coal transported by train from south Wales and wood obtained locally later removed the demand for peat. In pre-war days Newbridge had four paraffin powered street lights each of which consisted of a tall pole bearing a cross bar. The flames would flare six inches high producing a "good" light! One of these poles was still in use until fairly recently holding up a fence! When electricity did arrive it was supplied by a generator situated near the centre of the village and the quality of the supply depended on the diligence of the operator.

The water supply at this time was essentially local. The main supply originated at Schache Bank and a small reservoir on the Hirnant, a point west of the village. Water taps were shared, usually three households used one tap. A surplus tank existed and was situated in the Centre of the village where villagers could take their containers for extra water. Prior to this the Rock Well to the rear of the Sychnant housing estate provided much of the village's water needs.

In the early 1900's Newbridge had its own supply of electricity as did Llysdinam Hall. The "Power House" as it was known was situated in the centre of the village and was basically a shed containing the generator. The system required 1 man to operate it and the engines were driven by paraffin. Villagers were able to take their own batteries along to be charged.

Except for the soldiers who became casualties of the conflicts, the 1914-1918 and 1939-45 World Wars left few physical scars on the village. Newbridge did, however, play host to a considerable number of children evacuated from as far away as Bootle, London, Luton, Birmingham, Coventry, Birkenhead, Cardiff and Swansea.

A Photograph of the Newbridge & district soldiers who
returned from World War 1 in 1919.

In addition the Prisoner of War camp built at the north end of the village added to the village's awareness of the war. The camp housed some sixty prisoners, mostly Italian, who were sent out in gangs to work on farms in the local area.

The prisoner of war camp before it was
demolished in the late 1990s

The prisoners were renowned locally for their ability to "make rings out of 3d bits; cigarette lighters out of all sorts of scrap and when out draining to catch frogs for subsequent cooking!".

The end of the war brought a new era to the village. Tractors came and horses went from the farms. The first tractor and hydraulic plough was introduced to the village by Sir Charles Venables Llewelyn in 1939 for the 140 acres of ploughland on the Llysdinam Estate, although the waggoner and his horses were kept until 1944.

Post-war a sewage treatment plant was built and new council housing estates were developed at Gwaryffordd in 1950, Llwyncelyn in 1958 and Dolyfan in 1970 followed by a rash of private developments from the 1980's through the 1990's and into the new millennium all held in bounds until recently by the proposed route of the Newbridge bypass which has already waited over fifty years for its construction.

As a result of the Beeching cuts by 1962 the twin tracked line with two platforms, two waiting rooms, booking office, maintenance/shunting shed, signal box, weighbridge and store shed, which made up Newbridge on Wye Station were no more. No longer would the flour, coal, and cattle for the village, and ice for Llysdinam Hall travel by rail, but, almost as if in compensation, the new village school opened in the same year to offer new horizons to the new generation in Newbridge-on-Wye.

Newbridge and its Bridges

The Wye Bridge, Newbridge-on-Wye

The current reinforced concrete bridge was built in 1981 and although it could have been built as a single span it has 3 arches to link its design to the bridge it replaced.

In 1910/11 a three-span, deck-arch bridge itself replaced an old wooden bridge. It was one of the first examples of the use of ferro concrete in mid-Wales and a bridge unique of its type.

Much of the material for the bridge was of local origin. Gravel came from the river at Llyn Cam and although only a few hundred yards upstream it took three horses to pull the cart up the steep bank.

In-fill material for the 1911 bridge came from a quarry by the Estyn Brook and much of the stone facing was dressed on site by stone-masons.

The bridge was opened by Lady Venables-Llewelyn and her son George (who was then still young enough to be in a pram).

The bridge pre-1910 which dated from the 18th Century was a seven span wooden bridge with no masonry of any kind: it stood on six piles rammed down into the gravel bed of the river, the spaces in between the uprights being boarded over with oak and packed inside with heavy stones. These supports presented the least possible obstruction to the flow of water and suffered little damage from floods. The deck of the bridge was of oak planks overlaid with Macadam: the renewal of the decking proved a constant source of expense.

Though the bridge had sufficed for many generations, the coming of motor vehicles soon proved that it was inadequate for modern traffic and it was rebuilt at the joint expense of the Counties of Brecon and Radnor on a site alongside the old bridge.

Fragments of the old bridge are occasionally unearthed from the river bed.

Pont ar Ithon, Newbridge-on-Wye

The stone bridge to the south of the village carrying the A470 over the river Ithon was restored in 1934. The embankments to an earlier bridge can be seen on either bank some 100m downstream of the existing one.

The bridge is listed for renewal "at some time".

It had a bad reputation as an accident black spot, being only wide enough for one vehicle to pass over at a time, and even in the days of the horse, a tanker of paraffin capsized on it, the only casualty on that occasion being the horse. Today permanent traffic lights operate on the bridge and these have made it a much safer passing place.

Brynwern Bridge, Newbridge-on-Wye

Although the present concrete bridge dates only from 1980 it replaced a three-span lattice girder bridge erected in 1885 which was demolished despite being a grade II listing and the only remaining example of it's type on the Wye. It was engineered by Stephen Williams of Rhayader, the architect of Newbridge church and Doldowlod Hall, and built by William Thomas' Railway Foundry at Llanidloes for W. Clifton Mogg a retired clergyman who, at about the same time, had built nearby Brynwern Hall and required convenient access to it.

The former 3-span, lattice girder bridge at Brynwern

Footbridge on Llysdinam Estate

This was a suspension footbridge which connected the Penybont and Aberithon home farms on the Llysdinam Estate. Only remnants of the footings of the bridge still remain.

Ystrad Footbridge, Doldowlod Estate

An elegant suspension bridge built around 1880. The ironwork for this bridge was made at the Llanidloes Railway Foundry. The towers are nearly 4½ metres high and the length of the span between the towers is 42 metres. The deck width is 1.2 metres which made it wide enough to drive stock across the river but not for a vehicle or for a horse and cart.

In 1989 the bridge was completely dismantled and restored by Hope & Son Builders of Newbridge-on-Wye and it is now registered by the Institution of Civil Engineers as a National Heritage Structure.

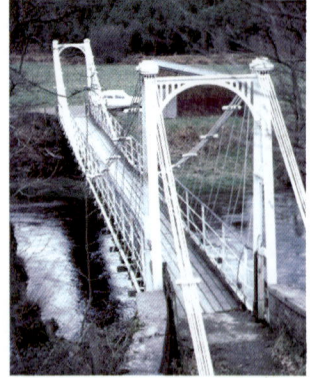

Railway Bridges

Both of the local railway river crossings have now gone, one having been over the mouth of the Ithon close to Brynwern and another, somewhat upstream of the present Wye (road) bridge known as "the Black Bridge". Both bridges were originally lattice-girder structures carried on timber piers but were encased in concrete during the 1920's. Very little evidence of their existence remains today but when the river Wye is low, the base of the sheet piling which was used when the cast-iron piers were encased in concrete are visible where the Black Bridge (pictured below) once stood.

Llysdinam

Over the river from Newbridge, in the old county of Breconshire, is the ancient parish of Llysdinam, once the home of the royal descendents of Brychan, Prince of Brycheiniog (the ancient word for Breconshire). The parish church was in ruins by the end of the 17th Century and now only the site remains on Penllys bank. Penllys was at one time the seat of justice for the area.

In Norman times, the top of Penllys bank was occupied by a defensive ringwork to control the ford on the most northern outpost of the Lordship of Buellt (Builth). It would have had a timber keep surrounded by a timber palisade and around it would have developed a small community of farmers and silk workers. Evidence for the cultivation of flax has been found in Newbridge itself so that it seems likely that, as elsewhere in Radnorshire, a linen industry also existed.

The parish next came to fame as an early centre of the Baptist church. The first Baptist leader was Hughes Evans of Llanyre and among the first congregations to be established was that of Thomas Evans at Pentre Farm, Llysdinam. Evans had been ejected from his living quarters at Maesmynis near Builth Wells when he would not subscribe to the Act of Uniformity of 1662. He then went to live at Pentre in Llysdinam, which after 1672 became a licensed meeting house, although worship during the summer months took place in a barn called Rhyd Galed and baptisms were conducted in the nearby Estyn Brook.

The Baptist Chapel built in the village in 1760 was called New Pentre or Pentre Neuadd in remembrance of the first meeting place of the congregation. This building was replaced in 1824 and again by the present chapel in 1880 (see photos – page 5).

In the seventeenth century Baptists were often persecuted and excommunicated from the church of England and even refused burial on church ground. A maid, who was a Baptist, died and was secretly buried in Llanfihangel Bruynpabuan graveyard. The priest had the coffin exhumed and dragged on a cart to the crossroads on the Llanafan road a mile or so from Newbridge where she was re-buried and even her gravestone there was smashed.

Thomas Huet, who was preceptor of St David's cathedral and Rector of Cefnllys and Disserth and who translated the book of Revelation into Welsh for the New Welsh Testament of 1567, built a house in the parish called Ty Mawr. This and many other properties in the parish passed through several families until the Llysdinam properties were acquired in 1827 by Archdeacon Richard Venables who came to live at the newly built Llysdinam Hall in about 1830.

Richard was a Fellow of Clare College, Cambridge before holding variously, and often concurrently, the posts of vicar of Clyro, Prebend of Llansantffraed, Archdeacon of Carmarthen, and vicar of Nantmel with Llanyre. In 1847 he resigned the parish of Clyro in favour of his eldest son Richard Lister Venables who also succeeded his father as Chairman of the Radnorshire Quarter Sessions and owner of Llysdinam Hall. R.L. Venables had spent 1837-8 in Russia with his first wife and on his return wrote "Domestic Scenes in Russia" which ran to two editions. It was Richard Lister's brother George Stovin Venables, a barrister and well known in the literary world who provided the money to build Newbridge church. A further, but then unknown, literary associate came with the appointment in 1865 of Francis Kilvert as curate at Clyro. Kilvert's diaries published after his death paint a beautiful picture of life in Wales at that time.

George Stovin Venables' first wife died and he married Agnes Minna Pearson, cousin of the Duchess of Norfolk and they had a daughter Katherine Minna. Kilvert was fond of both Mrs Venables and her young daughter and often recorded his visits to Llysdinam in his diaries. Katherine, born in may 1870, married Charles Leyshon Dillwyn-Llewelyn in August 1893 and the name of Venables was added after Dillwyn but before Llewelyn.

From the early 1800's the Dillwyn family owned the Nantgarw potteries in Swansea. L.W. Dillwyn developed the company but his interest in natural history, particularly botany and his election as a Fellow of the Royal Society in 1804 led him to leave the pottery in 1817. He married Mary Llewelyn of Penllergaer and his son John took her surname to become John Dillwyn Llewelyn. Like his father he became interested in botany and collaborated with Wheatstone on the electric telegraph and Fox Talbot (a relative by marriage) on photography. His son John Talbot Dillwyn Llewelyn married Caroline Hicks-Beach in 1861, was created a baronet in 1890 and, after the death of their first son, the younger son Charles Leyshon Dillwyn-Llewelyn born in 1870 became baronet in 1927, to be succeeded by his son Sir Michael in 1951. In 1934 Sir Michael married Lady Delia Mary Hicks Beach and their son John Dillwyn Venables Llewelyn is the present Baronet.

Llysdinam Hall, residence of the Dillwyn Venables-Llewelyn family.

All Saints Church, Newbridge-on-Wye

All Saints Church, Newbridge-on-Wye was built at the expense of George Stovin Venables of Llysdinam Hall at a cost of £4,600 and was consecrated on Thursday 12th July 1883. The architect was S.W. Williams of Rhayader and the stained glass was by C.E. Kempe, one of the best glass artists of the period whose signature of a wheatsheaf can be found in the first window on the north side. The exterior is in the Decorated or Middle Pointed Style. A marble mosaic in the sanctuary is in memory of Agnes Minna Venables who died in 1909 and most windows commemorate members of the Venables family.

The font is by John Ridley; the eagle lectern by Meyer of Munich and the choir stall panels carved by Agnes Minna Venables herself.

A memorial fountain to the first vicar John Edward Lloyd stands on the village green and is pictured below.

All Saints Church, Newbridge-on-Wye

Photograph showing interior of All Saints Church

The Old School at Newbridge

The old school masters house by the village green is all that remains of the school which served the village from 1868 to 1962 when the present school was opened. Its history is a direct reflection of the social history of the times.

Prior to the opening of the school the basic principles of reading, writing and arithmetic were taught to about 40 pupils in the unheated Baptist chapel using pew doors laid upon the tops of pews as desks. Henry Penry of Brecon visited this school on 2nd November 1846 as part of the Government's landmark Inquiry into the State of Education in Wales. Until this Inquiry was published in 1847 little was known of the subject and the effect was to spur the establishment of schools in rural areas and towns throughout Wales headed by school masters who had received some kind of training or degree. This Inquiry was one of two influential factors in the establishment of a school in the village. The other factor was the Venables family at Llysdinam Hall.

In the 1860's the Venables family of Llysdinam helped establish the new school in the village subsequently known as Newbridge School but officially, Llanyre National School. They signed a deed conveying the land formerly known as Green Cottage to the vicar and church wardens of the Parish of Llanyre for the purposes of a school:

> "…. for the education of children and adults of the labouring and other poorer classes in the parish of Llanyre or in any other adjoining parish within a radius of 3 miles from the village of Newbridge…"

Green Cottage was demolished and the red brick, one room School was erected. An adjoining house was built in readiness for the first school master.

Mr William Thomas was the first headmaster from its opening in January 1868 to December 1871. He was an experienced kind and patient disciplinarian who was an ideal person to get the school under way. His class rose in a few weeks from 36 to 80 scholars and the 45′ x 15′ room soon began to get crowded. In addition to children a few adults up to the age of 25 attended long enough to learn to sign their names and read simple documents.

The first entry in the school log book on 6th January 1868 read:-

"Commenced school this day at Newbridge. The building is entirely new. The opening ceremony took place on New Years Day when the school was declared open. 36 scholars were admitted today all of whom were very backward, only one child out of the above number could work addition of money and three could work easy sums in simple addition. As to notation and numeration, all were entirely ignorant; but this ignorance is not to be wondered at when it is know that no kind of school has been at Newbridge for some years."

The children were often needed to help on the farms. They were used for setting and harvesting potatoes and swedes, harvesting hay and corn, preparing birds for the Christmas markets, killing pigs in January, collecting acorns (mast) as pig food, barking oaks for tanning and during the hiring fairs. These fairs caused movement and disruption to the lives of servants thus making regular school attendance by their children very difficult. Until 1893 a child at the age of 10 could obtain partial or total exemption from school to work.

Prior to the building of the church the school was used for a Sunday School, church services, fortnightly "penny readings" and any other event which required accommodation in the village.

By November 1869 Mr Thomas was now single-handedly teaching some 96 children. The diarist the Rev. Francis Kilvert, curate of Clyro occasionally visited the school when he visited Richard Venables at Llysdinam, the vicar of Clyro. Rev. Kilvert visited the school around a dozen times in all. One log book entry on September 17th 1870 reads:

Class 1 of Newbridge
School 1905.

Senior Class of
Newbridge School 1897.

The second headmaster Mr George Roche Smith served 35 years in the school from 1872 to 1907. His wife taught sewing and in their turn his three daughters became pupil teachers but the intense pressure of the job undoubtedly hastened the premature death of at least one. Mr Smith was a strict disciplinarian and soon broke the children of the habit of arriving late and unwashed. Several pupils walked over four miles to school, in winter starting before daylight, and were allowed an extra 10 minutes to arrive provided the time was made up in the lighter months. Within five years attendance was 160 with four classes in one room.

Disease not infrequently closed the school, whooping cough, measles, chicken pox, mumps, diptheria, scarlet fever, typhoid, jaundice, ringworm, conjunctivitis and influenza were all common diseases.

On February 26th 1892 Mr Smith reported four village children dead of whooping cough, by March 11th ten were dead and by the 16th, 16 children in the village, almost a tenth of the child population had died of the disease within a month.

Mr Smith was succeeded by four headmasters who carried the school through the first half of the twentieth century. They were: Mr J.R.L. Clevely (1907-1913); Mr E. Evans (1913-1925); Captain A. Logan (1925-1931) and Mr G.J. Thomas (1932-1962). All these men witnessed great changes both in education and in the village, making the school an integral part of the history of the village itself.

The old school eventually closed after 94½ years in the summer of 1962. The last head master of the old school, Mr G.J. Thomas also resigned when the school closed. His final entry in the school log book read:-

"School closes today after very many years. The new school opens on September 4th. Mrs M.J. Williams retires with effect from 31st August, 1962.

I relinquish this headship after a fairly long pull. My retirement is with effect from 31st August, 1962. I wish the new Head Master a long and happy time."

The new school, Newbridge-on-Wye V.P. (Voluntary Primary) School opened its doors on September 4th 1962 as a Church in Wales School and it was a far cry from the old establishment. It had a modern central heating system, a large hall to be used as a canteen or for school concerts, etc.. It had a large playground for the children and employed a gardener for the upkeep of it's sizeable gardens. The new headmaster was Mr Vincent Hill and the school was officially opened on 2nd November 1962 by Lady Delia Venables-Llewelyn. A new Community Centre was built adjacent to the school in 1987.

Around Newbridge

The Railway Community at Builth Road

Between the years of 1864 and 1963, Newbridge had a railway service transporting people, supplies and animals through the village. The Mid-Wales Railway Line arrived at Newbridge in 1864 when the Llanidloes to Brecon section was opened. At Llanidloes it joined with the Llanidloes and Newtown Railway and the two formed the branch line which ran for nearly a century from Moat Lane to Brecon.

The present Builth Road station is situated where the railway line from Shrewsbury to Swansea crossed over that from Moat Lane to Brecon. It stood in Llanelwedd parish but in 1886 the new church of St John the Divine Cwmbach Llechryd was opened and the parish of Cwmbach Llechryd was established to serve the community of around 50 houses which grew up around Builth Road because the railways ran through.

When the Mid-Wales Railway first opened in 1864 there was no station at Builth Road. All the M.W.R. maintenance and servicing facilities were sited at Builth Wells.

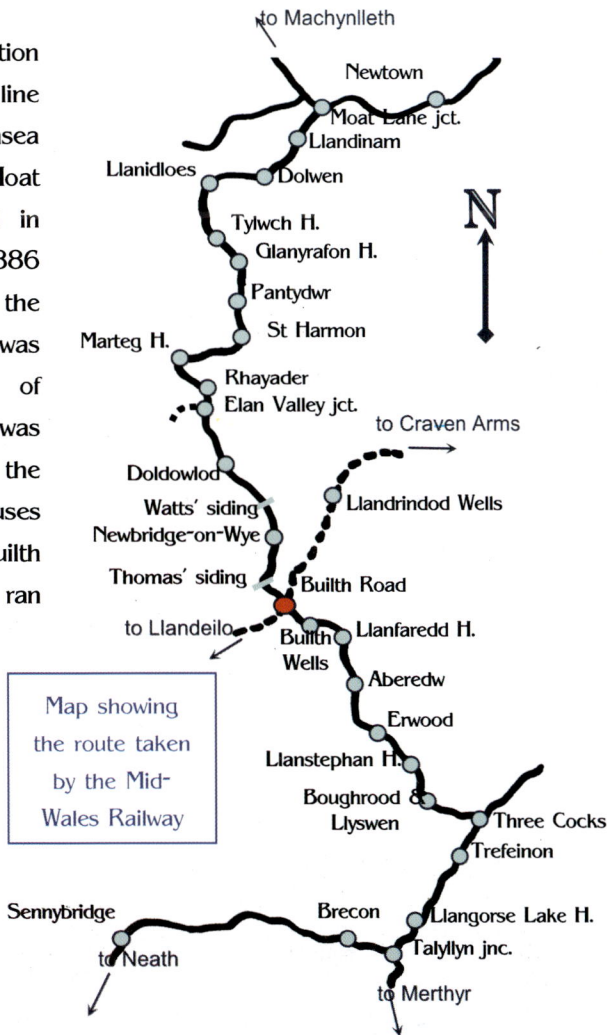

to Machynlleth

Newtown

Moat Lane jct.

Llandinam

Llanidloes

Dolwen

Tylwch H.

Glanyrafon H.

N

Pantydwr

Marteg H.

St Harmon

Rhayader

Elan Valley jct.

to Craven Arms

Doldowlod

Watts' siding

Llandrindod Wells

Newbridge-on-Wye

Thomas' siding

Builth Road

to Llandeilo

Builth
Wells

Llanfaredd H.

Aberedw

Map showing
the route taken
by the Mid-
Wales Railway

Erwood

Llanstephan H.

Boughrood &
Llyswen

Three Cocks

Trefeinon

Sennybridge

Brecon

Llangorse Lake H.

to Neath

Talyllyn jnc.

to Merthyr

The second railway to reach Builth Road was the Central Wales Extension Railway (CWER) which in 1865 extended the Central Wales Railway from Craven Arms through Knighton as far as Llandrindod Wells, finally reaching Llandovery in 1868 where it joined the Llanelli Railway. The C.W.E.R. became the L.N.W.R. (or London and North Western Railway) and on 1st November 1866 Builth Road High Level station was opened.

In 1867 the Mid Wales Railway opened its own station at Builth Road and was known as "Llechryd" until 1889 when it became "Builth Road Low-Level." At this time a loop line was laid allowing interchange of traffic between the high and low-level lines. Until the nationalisation of the railways in 1948 the high and low-level stations at Builth Road were virtually entirely separate concerns with separate staff.

The railway community at Builth Road was almost wholly L.N.W.R. Early on, a second platform was built at the high-level station with a long section of double track as far as the end of the loop line coming up from the Cambrian line and in 1871 an engine shed and turntable were erected.

The largest source of employment was the maintenance depot at which as many as seventy men were employed during the 1920's. The depot was nicknamed 'Dartmoor' and had offices, a sawmill, shops and stores for the multitude of tradesmen employed there. There were over one hundred men employed at Builth Road high-level alone. As well as living in the actual railway houses some men lived in the nearby cottages, many of which belonged to the Pencerrig estate, and about twenty men regularly cycled to work from Builth Wells.

Builth Wells Station, on 9th July 1959 showing 46512 on 5.08 Brecon – Moat Lane

Photograph: W.A.Camwell

Running behind the station was Railway Terrace. By around 1886 there were 13 houses in this long terrace. The houses in Wye View Terrace were built in two rows in the early 1890's by a contractor from Birmingham and are numbered 18-42. Good quality water was brought from a spring two miles in the direction of Howey and supplied through outside standpipes arranged strategically outside the blocks. The houses all had gardens and many residents had allotments and most families kept a pig. Bakers and butchers from Newbridge-on-Wye and Builth regularly called. Visits to Builth for shopping by train were very easy. The estate was very well kept but over the years the houses tended to become old fashioned; electricity did not arrive until 1949 and running water and modern drainage for each house did not follow for another ten years or so.

Following the outbreak of the First World War, some staff and their sons were called away to fight and both railway lines had to handle very heavy traffic. After the war the eight-hour day was introduced. This had a huge impact on the way the 2 railways were run and greatly stepped up working costs without any increase in revenue.

Entering Newbridge

Photograph: W A Camwell.

By the 1930's conditions were becoming difficult for the railways. There was heavy competition from road transport, although the local effects were partly cushioned by the increase in traffic in roadstone from the nearby quarries of Builth and Rhayader which the county councils were using for a vast programme of road improvements. This competition coupled with the cutbacks in coal and iron production in south Wales meant that the depot at Builth Road began to feel the effects.

With the onset of the Second World War, a great upsurge in traffic on the railway lines meant that they were again working at their full capacity. This effect lasted until the mid 1950's when the lifting of fuel rationing meant a great increase in the volume of road traffic. The railways were nationalised from 1st January 1948. Under the Beeching "Axe" in November 1962 the whole of the network from Moat Lane via Builth to Brecon, with the associated route to Hereford was completely closed. The last real use made of the loop line was in connection with the recovery of track and materials from the M.W.R. line.

The houses were sold to a property company, 'Drum Estates' which then sold them on and they have now been converted into private homes. The building of the high-level station has been converted into three dwelling houses and the old refreshment room and its house on the low-level have now become the Cambrian Arms, a free house, which contains a number of interesting railway relics.

The last train on the MWR Line, December 1962.

The birth and death of the Cambrian railway are encompassed by the life of the late John Jones the tailor of Llanwrthwl, and a popular local singer. To celebrate his 102nd birthday he took a trip on the line, on which he could remember seeing the first train 97 years previously. The line, which ran through some of the most scenic parts of the countryside, was closed following the Beeching Report in 1962. The line that had taken over five years to lay, and had lasted 100 years was dismantled and removed in only a few months. The last passenger train ran on a cold December day in 1962.

Pencerrig School & St. John's Church, Cwmbach Llechryd

Penccerrig School, Cwmbach was opened in 1865 and was built at the expense of Mrs Thomas of Pencerrig. It was considerably enlarged in the 1890's, just at the time the number of railway workers was rising dramatically. By the early 1900's the school had over 120 pupils and four teachers. When the County School opened at Llandrindod, it became possible for bright children to enjoy secondary education, travel by train from Builth Road was simple and convenient. By the 1930's numbers at Pencerrig School were falling and the staff was reduced to two teachers, this was partly due to the opening of Oxford Road School in Llandrindod where the children could again travel simply by train. Some older girls also had cookery lessons at Llanelwedd school.

The parish church of St John opened in 1886. The cost of this scheme was £12,000 and was borne by Miss Clara Thomas of Pencerrig, the daughter of Mrs Thomas who had been responsible for the erection of the school.

The first vicar of the new parish of Cwmbach was the Reverend Mr Welby, who is mentioned as a locum at Clyro in Kilvert's Diary. He was followed in 1893 by the Reverend John Lonsdale Bryans, M.A. who served here for over 40 years. Nonconformists were catered for by services held in the waiting room of the low-level station and later in a mission church erected at the bottom of the station-master's garden.

St. Cewydd's Church, Disserth

A mile and a half out of Newbridge on the minor road to Howey, Disserth Church nestles on the banks of the river Ithon and is well worth a visit. The church is dedicated to St Cewydd who has other more or less local dedications at Aberedw and Cusop. Tradition has it that he belongs to the 6th Century and was one of the so-called Sons of Gildas, a group of monks who travelled south from Strathclyde, founding churches *en route* and eventually finding their way to Brittany.

The River Ithon flows by for baptisms and the daily needs of those who settled here. The site is hidden from view and had a better chance of escaping the unwanted attentions of raiders and marauders.

Disserth is largely a 13th Century church with a good tower. It is solid and defensive in style, surmounted with battlements and splayed at the base in the style of a military building of that period.

Inside the Church there is a spiral staircase giving access to the belfry where one of its three bells dates from the early 14th Century. The nave and chancel are large for the size of the parish and are all under one roof in traditional Radnorshire style and belong to the mid-15th Century. The outside walls are whitewashed with the exception of the tower. Inside the stone font is octagonal on a round base and is medieval. No stained glass has survived at Disserth. Most of the windows are wood framed and of simple design, though the south wall of the chancel has a three light window with trefoiled heads in stone.

The place name Disserth, which occurs elsewhere in Wales, as well as in Cornwall and Ireland, commemorates the "desert place", beloved of Celtic saints as offering suitable sites for their churches.

Although most of the medieval church was very colourful with stained glass windows now all gone, there are some remnants of 15th Century wall decoration on the east wall of the chancel which were exposed in 1954. These are similar to that found in other medieval churches.

The niche in the wall behind the altar may originally have housed some kind of statue or object of devotion which disappeared at the Reformation. The church is furnished with box pews each with high sides and a door with the names of their "rightful" occupants.

Look out in Disserth for the pews of James Watt and his son, also James Watt.

Legend has it and the same story is told for several churches in mid-Wales – that to lay an evil spirit the parson, armed with book and candle summoned the spirit to appear and by prayer and denunciation reduced the spirit to the size of a bluebottle fly, put it in a snuff box and put the box where it could never emerge – in this case in the bog at Cors y Llyn just south of Newbridge.

Edward Llwyd told an interesting story in his Parochialia of 1696 about St. Cewydd's Well at Disserth. This is what he wrote:-

"In ye parish of Disserth, Radnorshire, a woman told me that she us'd every new years-dayy (after she had filled her pitcher) to drwssio'r fynnawn (dress the well) with misselto. She that first came to the well after midnight honno kai crop y fynnawn, rhaid drwsio'r fynnawn, hi kai fod yn bhrenioes (would received the crop of the well, the well must be dressed, she would be a queen); they yt came after had none of ye vertue."

An eighteenth century traveller on his way to Llandrindod Wells described how at Disserth:

"The churchyard, which though large, was filled with people of almost all ages and qualities. The church is a strong building and pretty large, against the tiles of which were a dozen lusty fellows playing at tennis and as many against the steeple at fives. On one side of the church were about six couples dancing to one violin and just below three or four couples to three violins, whose seat was on a tombstone. In short, the whole was something whimsically odd. Here we saw common games of ball played against the sacred pile and there was also music playing over the bodies of the deceased."

According to the traveller's account these Disserth revellers "spoke as almost everyone else did, in the Welsh tongue.". Likewise in 1744 some other travellers met:

> "... a man with a sledge or car on which he had a cask of ale drawn by one horse. This is the common way here of transporting from one place to another. The man told Mr Percy, *in Welsh* that he was going to Disserth Wake, a village about two miles off."

Disserth Church today looks almost entirely as it did in the late 18th Century. The reasons for this could be that in 1883 the Chapel of Ease at Betws Disserth was rebuilt and in 1887 Betws Disserth was separated from Disserth parish and annexed to that of Llansanffraid-yn-Elfael. Furthermore in 1887 another portion of Disserth parish was assigned to the new parish of Cwmbach Llechryd created to serve the needs of the growing railway community at Builth Road. This coupled with the growing popularity of nonconformity made Disserth a low priority to the Victorians This could perhaps go some way towards explaining why Disserth Church pretty much "escaped" too much Victorian alteration.

Disserth church is a favourite building for Natterers, Pipistrelle and Long Eared bats but fear not – if you do! – for they are not about by day, however, "mouse droppings" on the pews provide evidence of their night time patrols.

Pipistrelle Bat

Doldowlod

About 3 miles north of Newbridge-on-Wye stands Doldowlod Hall, a fine Victorian mansion in a superb position facing south across the Wye valley. The house is best viewed from the Wye Valley Walk on Trembydd Hill opposite.

Doldowlod or "Doledowlod", perhaps meaning "the meadow with the barn" was part of a parcel of 6 farms and a corn mill bought in 1803 by James Watt, the famous inventor and steam engineer, from Penry Price, a local landowner. There is a pleasant story in several histories and guide books to Radnorshire that Watt found the property when travelling in the area, liked it and bought it. This is untrue. Watt had never visited the area before 1803, but wished to buy land after his retirement from his steam engine business in Birmingham.

Portrait of James Watt, Senior, 1736-1818 (Banks Archive)

The estate was found for him by his land agent, James Crummer (who later built Howey Hall), and bought "on liking" -- i.e. subject to Mr Watt's approval on viewing. Watt together with his son James Watt Junior then came to have a look, liked the estate, disliked the owner ("...of all the lying shuffling drunken rascals I have met...., but my lawyers say his titles are good") and bought it. In 1803 Doldowlod was an ordinary farm – the farmhouse stood where the northern half of the Hall now stands.. Watt himself lived in Birmingham and only visited the estate on a few occasions before his death in 1819.

James Watt Senior was too old to ride long distances on horseback and the roads were bad so that carriage travel was slow and uncomfortable. He seems never to have stayed in the farmhouse, preferring the Red Lion in Rhayader, although he took a keen interest in the management of the estate ("The tenant at Doldowlod is ruining both himself and the farm, his crops are miserable and his hay good for nothing" (1805). Between 1803 and 1819 he bought many more local farms, in particular those around and across the river from Doldowlod. James Watt Junior, however, liked Doldowlod very much and stayed there regularly from about 1806 onwards although his home and business remained in Birmingham.

He used to ride over from Birmingham on horseback, taking two days over the journey. On one famous occasion in 1813 he and his horse fell into the bog at Llandegly and had to be pulled out: "He sunk suddenly up to his belly and I to my boot tops in disengaging myself."). It was he who over the next 40 years built up the Doldowlod Estate, planted most of the now mature oaks and beeches in the valley between Doldowlod and Newbridge, laid out the main grounds and the gardens and built the present extensive stone outbuildings and the south (down-river) section of the Hall.

James Watt Junior started building the Hall in about 1843, supervising the work himself and relying on an architect friend, Robert Mylne, for the detailed designs. He demolished the old farm buildings and built the Hall onto the south end of the old farmhouse, which was used as the kitchens and servants' quarters and remained where the north half of the Hall now stands until 35 years later. Much of the attractive design of the Hall — the pointed gable features, the chimneys, the design of the windows — reflects Aston Hall in Birmingham (right), a fine red-brick Jacobean (1639) house in which Watt Junior lived

from 1818 until his death The fine woodwork in the Hall is local oak. The source of the stone is not known precisely.

James Watt Junior never married and had no children. On his death in 1848 he left all his property to his great-nephew (his sister Margaret's grandson) James Watt Gibson, on condition that he took the surname Watt. James Watt Gibson Watt (as he became) made his home at Doldowlod and after marrying quite late in life he built the second half of the Hall in 1877-8. This involved demolishing the old farmhouse, replacing it with the northern half of the present Hall and also extending the south face of the Hall into the hill behind.

The front staircase and the front entrance were both moved and re-designed. The terraced lawns in front of the house were created at this time, probably with the rubble from the farmhouse and the residues from dressing the new stone on site. The architect is understood to have been Stephen Williams of Rhayader, who designed Newbridge-on-Wye Church and several other fine local churches. The stonework and design are so well matched that it is impossible to tell that the two halves of the Hall were built 50 years apart.

The old kitchens at the back of the Hall were demolished in 1949 and various changes have been made to the grounds, the terrace and the layout of the gardens, but otherwise the Hall remains much as it was in 1880.

James Watt Gibson Watt died in 1891.

He is buried at Llanyre Church which he took a leading role in rebuilding. This fine monument stands there in his memory.

Major J.M. Gibson Watt was the next to inherit Doldowlod and served, after university, in the Life Guards and South Wales borders and in 1911 married Marjorie Ricardo of Gatcombe in Gloucestershire. Until his death in 1929 he was a county councillor and J.P. two offices subsequently held by his widow who also ran the Doldowlod estate until 1946.

Her son David Gibson Watt married Diana Hambro in 1942. He served in the Welsh Guards until 1946 and she was a nurse and ambulance driver throughout the war. After the war he went into local government and in 1956 became M.P. for Hereford. He served in the House of Commons for 19 years finishing as Minister of State at the Welsh Office. He was awarded a life peerage as Lord Gibson-Watt of Wye in 1979.

Doldowlod Station was about three miles south of Rhayader on the Mid-Wales Railway. It served Doldowlod Estate and Llanwrthwl. A private siding ("Watts Siding") served the estate and was used principally for transporting timber.

The picture above shows Doldowlod Station formerly Cambrian Raiways looking North, 9th July 1959 showing 46522 entering on the 9.55 am Moat Lane – Brecon. The signal box here was closed during the week ending 6th June 1962 and all trains then used the down platform i.e. the east side of the station.

Quotations from the letters of James Watt and James Watt Junior on pages 41-44 are taken from the Doldowlod Papers now in Birmingham Reference Library. Copyright Birmingham City Council.

Church of St. Llyr, Llanyre

The small village of Llanyre lies about 2 km to the west of Llandrindod Wells and 5km north-east of Newbridge. The Church is dedicated to St. Llyr, a Saint who lived towards the end of the 5th Century. A document dated from 1566 refers to "Llanllyr-on-Rhos" which, coupled with the shape of the churchyard, points to an early medieval origin.

The medieval church was reported to have had an unusual, ornate roof consisting of a single-cell nave and chancel which was said to similar to that at Llanfihangel Helygen. (2½ km to the north). Documents dating from around 1805 imply the church was rebuilt around that date, although there is no other evidence to corroborate this. Williams, in 1818 described the church as "a humble structure, consisting of a nave, chancel and low tower." At that time the base of the rood screen remained in place, and the belfry was only a partitioned part of the western bay and contained a parish chest hollowed out of a single trunk. The distinctive remnants of a curvilinear churchyard are still to be seen within the later walled yard.

With predominant funding by James Watt-Gibson-Watt, the church was entirely rebuilt by S.W. Williams in 1885-7. A brass plaque commemorates it's reopening by James Watt-Gibson-Watt's wife in 1885. The New Church retains little from its predecessor except for the font.

St. Afan's Church, Llanafan Fawr

Llanafan Fawr is thought to have once been the mother church for the area. The churchyard morphology together with the dedication to St Afan denote an early medieval beginning for the site. The OS map marks the location of St Afan's tomb to the south of the south-east angle of the present chancel. This is said to date to the 14th century. At the beginning of the 20th century it was recorded as standing 7ft high and being surrounded by a drystone wall. The church stands on a raised oval platform some 50m in diameter which may be the remains of an earlier smaller churchyard or even a contemporary inner enclosure.

Part of the medieval church survives and it contains several interesting features, most notably several early medieval stone fragments and a pillar stone. The tower was rebuilt in 1765. By 1887 the church was in an almost a ruin. The tower was renovated, the chancel demolished and the church rebuilt on a smaller scale by S. W. Williams. The north and east walls of the nave and chancel were retained, but new windows were inserted, the old chancel was demolished with the new chancel formed at the east end of existing nave. The south wall was completely rebuilt and the porch was taken down and rebuilt in 1887.

The churchyard is massive and would originally have been nearly circular. On the west and south it has been squared off to make room for minor roads and suchlike. There are localised concentrations of monuments but generally the graves and their memorials are well spread across the south side of the churchyard. There are also a few to the east of the old chancel but none on the west and north.

St. Michael's Church, Llanfihangel Brynpabuan

St Michael's church lies on a spur about two miles to the south-west of Newbridge-on-Wye in the northern part of the old county of Breconshire and is aligned south-west/north-east.

The core of the Church is said to be 13th Century but the church itself has had considerable Victorian restoration, and only a stoup and a font from its medieval fittings remain. The windows except for the ground level window on the south wall were replaced by C. Buckeridge in 1868 along with the numerous other repairs.

The churchyard at Llanfihangel is an irregular polygon with one side - the south-east - faintly curved. The ground within the churchyard is flattish, though there is a gentle slope down in the northern sector.

The monuments are concentrated to the south and south-west of the church but they are sparse and predominantly 19th and 20th Century.

Inside the south-eastern perimeter of the churchyard is a low scarp. There is at least a possibility that this is the original boundary to an enclosure and that the hollow beyond is an accompanying ditch.

Castell Collen, Roman Fort

The Roman fort at Castell Collen (NGR SO 0562) is about 1.6 km north west of Llandrindod Wells. It formed the most important feature in the Roman defence of central Wales. The site was ideal as the loop of the river Ithon provides natural defences round an elevated spur which gave a commanding position with good drainage.

Castell Collen was originally constructed in AD 75-78 by Julius Frontinus as part of his campaign against the Silures (the Latin name for the local tribes-people who lived here at the time). Although it was an auxiliary fort, evidence exists that proves that the 2nd Augustan Legion visited the site, (travelling from Caerleon in South Wales) in the latter part of the 2nd Century AD. They were involved in a massive programme of rebuilding at the site, which included revetting the turf and timber defences with stone and erecting huge stone semi-circular gate-towers. Castell Collen then became the prototype for this type of monumental fort construction.

The improved fort defences were so successful, and presumably the local Silurians were so intimidated, that early in the 3rd Century AD the fort was dramatically reduced in size. Originally it would have held an auxiliary unit of 1000 men in a mixed cavalry and infantry unit (*cohors equitata*). The number of troops would have been reduced to about 500 men with the reduction in the size of the fort. This peace was of a temporary nature, and the defences and gates were renewed some 75 years later in the late 3rd or early 4th Century by Constantinus Chlorus. However, these were much reduced compared to the original scale of the fort. The story of Castell Collen ends here with the subsequent abandonment of the fort as the power of the Roman empire faded. The disused fort was raided for stone, which appears in other, local buildings, e.g. in the fabric of the chapel at Capel Maelog. The famous Log Boat in Llandrindod Wells Museum found in the River Ithon near the site, was possibly sunk during a raid on the fort at about this time.

The excavations
at Castell Collen
in 1957.

Llyn Gwyn

Llyn Gwyn lies about 4.8 km north of Newbridge (NGR SO 011652), and is a lake of legend and mystery. In legend it has been associated with Gwyn, king of the fairies and lord of the underworld and with the story of the "Croaking Trout." It is said that this lake was used by the monks of Abbeycwmhir to supply the abbey with fish. When the abbey was destroyed at the Reformation a monk came to the lake and prayed that every trout caught there from then on should cry out with abhorrence at the wrong which had been done. Since that day it is said that every trout caught makes a croaking noise and it became known as the lake of the croaking trout – fish which local people refused to eat.

The Mystery of the lake also surrounds nearby ancient earth works which some say are connected with the monks and others that they are the remains of the baths of the Roman garrison at Caer Fagu some two miles to the east and itself an outpost of the Roman Fort at Castell Collen near Llandrindod Wells.

Newbridge and Natural History

To the casual observer the countryside can appear to be deceptively unchanging but that is far from true. Around Newbridge as elsewhere, the 20th Century saw the horse replaced by the tractor, cereals and vegetables for home consumption replaced by permanent pasture, potent chemicals introduced to control plant and animal pests, hay replaced by silage and in the early 21st century the general demise of the dairy industry. With such a degree of change within agriculture, combined with acidification of our rivers by airborne pollution from distant industries and the detrimental effects of vastly increased road traffic, there can be little surprise that the natural history of this part of mid-Wales has also changed and generally for the worse. Very little of this change has been documented. When told that Globe Flowers are very rare in the general area and restricted in the village to a small island in the river the response from a member of a local WI that "When I was a girl 50 years ago we used to take armfuls to school - they were everywhere" sums up the fact that we often do not notice things are going until they are almost gone. A look back at the Game Books which record the shooting record on Llysdinam land give one of the few written glimpses of the way the area has changed. Shooting on their land at Upper Chapel in August 1911 the bag included grouse, black game, corncrake, partridge, snipe and teal. Today only the last two are at all common, the corncrake has not been heard in the area for decades and the other species have suffered virtual local extinction.

Globeflower

But everything in the Newbridge bird-world is not as bad as this, indeed lean over the Wye bridge at Newbridge and on a good day you might well see almost all the river birds of Wales within binocular view: Mallard, Heron, Goosander (a relative newcomer), Cormorant, Kingfisher, Dipper, Grey Wagtail and Sandpiper with Swallow, House and a few Sand Martins skimming flies off the summer river. Over recent years in spring and autumn Ospreys on their way to Scotland occasionally fly over and sometimes stay long enough to take a fish from the river.

In the river itself things have also changed. An old employee of Llysdinam House recalled that 40 years ago his wife would ask for a brace of wild Brown Trout for tea and within a few minutes of fishing tea would be in the bag. Similarly in the heyday of the river 300 salmon might be caught in a season on this section of the Wye.

Today Brown Trout are stocked and seasons can now pass with hardly a salmon caught although with patience an occasional autumn salmon may be seen swimming under the bridge going upstream to breed.

The other two rare fish which migrate upstream in summer to breed, the Allis and Twaite Shad, make few appearances in the Newbridge area.

In high summer the sea lamprey makes this same upstream journey to breed as its ancestors must have done since before dinosaurs roamed the land. The sea lamprey is the size of a large eel but its smaller relative the Brook Lamprey is only the size of a pencil, lives all its life in the river and as an adult does not feed but uses its sucker-like, jawless mouth to simply build its breeding nest - it also occurs near the river bridge but you are unlikely to see it. One fish which seems to be doing well in the river is the Grayling which in clear water may be spotted by its bluey-purple lips.

At the net and jam jar level of children's fishing the stony bottom of the river is likely to produce the Bullhead (or more aptly named Miller's Thumb), Stone Loach, Minnows and young Trout and Salmon. Another children's favourite, the lobster-like freshwater crayfish used to occur in the Newbridge reach of the River Ithon but siltation filled up its habitat between the stones of the riverbed and it disappeared. Although still found in tributaries from Cwmbach downstream crayfish have catastrophically declined in numbers all down the river in the last decade due to siltation, sheep dip and a disease called crayfish plague.

If the river has a special mammal then it must be the otter. This animal neared extinction in much of the UK in the 1960s due to pesticides. The mid-Wye was one of its few pesticide safe refuges. Unlike two of its favourite foods, crayfish and eels which are both in severe decline, the otter is on the up and up with their populations having now spread out from their Welsh, Lake District and South-west England refuges to recolonise most of their former range in England and Wales, helped in part by the release of captive bred stock.

For the last decade Newbridge has been the place where most dead (usually road casualty) otters have been sent for post-mortem, so this quiet corner of Wales has been in part responsible for monitoring its return.

Today the otter is fully protected and is even provided with artificial holts (homes) (there is one in Newbridge but you will not find it). However, otters much prefer to live under the root systems of riverside trees. An otter probably swims under the Wye bridge at Newbridge several times a week but being an animal of the dusk and night you are unlikely to see it, what you can find are its black, fish-scale filled droppings called spraint underneath the bridge. Beware, however, to the untrained spraint spotter otter and mink droppings can be confused as both are found on the river. Sometimes it is possible to identify the footprints of otters where they leave the water because of their five webbed toes, but again be careful if you find a five toed footprint near the water as this may be a badger coming down to drink.

Badgers like sloping ground in which to make their setts and on some higher river banks these great earth bowls, often covered with discarded grassy bedding are quite conspicuous as are their territory marking dung pit areas where a curl of black digested earthworm droppings are left in a collection of cereal bowl sized holes.

There are some other furry mammals which operate the night shift over the river and these are the bats. Without the help of modern bat detector technology to help it can be difficult to tell some of the species apart but the small bats close to the river are a mixture of Pipestrelles, of which probably more than a thousand breed within the wider village "fly zone", and the Daubenton's bat which is adapted to scoop insects off the river surface.

The big bat with a one foot (30cm) wingspan flying a treetop height up and down the river will be a Noctule (right – in a bat box at Llysdinam) and elsewhere in the vicinity will be Brown Long-eared, Whiskered, Brandt's, Natterers and who knows, but the very rare Barbastelle may even appear as it was found just below Builth Wells in 2003.

The river is not the only water-dominated habitat in and around the village for there are several peatlands once used as peat-cutting areas (turbaries) for fuel for the village. To the north of the village is the Vedw turbary now largely overgrown with Sallow and surrounded by rough grazing, with, to the south, the Aberithon turbary shown on maps as The Bog which is now a Site of Special Scientific Interest and across the Ithon is Cors y Llyn National Nature Reserve, a very special site indeed. Such boggy places are full of wildlife, not just the Teal, Water Rail, Sedge Warblers and Reed Buntings of the Reed and Sallow mix at Aberithon but the fascinating plants which make up these peatlands, not always spectacular in appearance but models of adaptation to a hostile environment.

Go through the marginal woodland (carr) at Cors y Llyn (which lies about 2 miles south of Newbridge off the A470) where grow Bog Bean and Bottle Sedge which once formed the vegetation mat which overgrew the "Llyn" (lake) to form the mat of floating vegetation creating the present quaking bog or "schwingmoor".

As you emerge along the boardwalk on to the open bog you enter a Bog Moss or Sphagnum dominated environment, saturated with water and as acidic as vinegar. Anything living here must be adapted not only to the acid environment but to the fact that only nutrient poor rainwater can reach the raised central area. Sphagnum copes by grabbing any nutrients in the rain and "exchanging" them for acidic ions ensuring that it keeps the area hostile to competitors. Also present at the bog edge is the tall moss Polytrichum (above). Some plants have found a way to overcome this nutrient deficiency. Round leafed Sundew (right) leaves, are covered in minute sticky tentacles, as a fly trap, digesting any caught insects to supplement its meagre diet. Back on Cors y Llyn take the time to look at some of the other plants. There is just one grass, the Flying Bent or Purple Moorgrass which grows in clumps

near the bog edge and, although it loses its leaves in winter, it moves all the nutrients from its leaves to its roots before the winter winds show how it got its name. The Cotton Sedges are very conspicuous when they are in flower, their white woolly heads being visible at considerable distances, and in autumn their red leaves illustrate why Wales has so many "Red Bogs" (Cors Goch). But take a look at the broad-leaved plants they are dominated by just one family, the heathers. There is Heather itself, Cross-leafed Heath, Crowberry and Cranberry all with water saving leaf characters which you might associate with plants of very dry areas such as waxy or hairy leaf surfaces and leaves rolled up with water losing pores on the inside. In fact these plants cannot use their roots to get water and nutrients directly from this acid and airless soil so they hold on tightly to what they have and rely upon fungi associated with their roots to do the rest.

There is another inconspicuous plant living on the fine branches of bog-side Birches which has an interesting history.

A small brown lichen (*Cetraria sepincola*, pictured above) known only outside Scotland from Cors y Llyn and a few similar local sites seems to have held on in this very short term twiggy environment since the last Ice Age 10,000 years ago!

Pollen analysis has been done on the site and revealed much about the local climate and environment over many millennia. Notably the discovery of *Humulus* (or Hops!) from the Roman period — perhaps the Romans brewed their own ale to keep out the cold British weather! Other pollen discoveries at the site include Cannabis (Hemp) and Flax. People possibly soaked the flax in the bog to strengthen it in order to make cloth for smocks and other garments.

After all this watery talk, the village area is quite well endowed with drier yet nevertheless exciting habitats. In some parts of Britain a "good" old meadow only needs to contain 50 - 70 species of flowering plant. Here in mid-Wales the threshold is much higher and to be "good" an old meadow here needs to contain at least 100 species of flowering plants, and the Newbridge examples do just that. What surprises many people when they first visit such an old meadow, particularly in summer, is that it is the broadleaved plants and not the grasses which predominate.

In the days of the horse most meadows would have been rich with wild flowers but today these herb rich old pastures are becoming a rarity. A couple of those that remain, within a mile or so of Newbridge, include one that has said to be arguably the best old meadow left in the UK. The best documented of these meadows is the one which borders Cors y Llyn. There is a public footpath through the site but to venture away from that requires a permit from the Countryside Council for Wales.

Cors y Llyn meadow in June is a sea of lilac Heath Spotted Orchids (right) interspersed with single red flowers of the almost spineless Meadow Thistle and the yellow spikes of a miniature broom-like plant Dyers' Greenweed (below).

Search these sites and other species rarely found in conventional grasslands will be seen such as Saw-wort, Wood Bitter Vetch, (left), (look for a clump on the road verge almost opposite the village green), Petty Whin and partially parasitic plants such as Eyebright, Red Bartsia, Yellow Rattle and Lousewort.

Every plant has its insect attendants, just think of cabbages in the garden or the 500 or so insects which are associated with Oak, and with over a hundred types of flowering plant, and taking into account the insects hunting other insects and the bugs of the soil, including the Yellow Ants which make conspicuous ant hills in old meadows, then the range of life, or the biodiversity to use a modern term, of these old meadows is amazing.

For comparison just count how many plants and insects you can see in a typical sheep-grazed improved pasture and I would be surprised if you even run out of fingers!

The visible countryside is generally the result of the social and economic history of an area. The economic changes due to changing agricultural practice have already been mentioned but equally important is the fact that along the Wye many of the large estates were established as much to give their owners access to exclusive fishing on one of the best salmon rivers in England and Wales and copses in which to shoot at other times as for any other reason. The wooded nature of the countryside gives an important added dimension to the natural history of the area.

Botanically the woodlands are Oak with mixtures of Alder and Ash but are not particularly exciting except to the lichen specialist or for the local abundance of Bird Cherry. Most of the interest lies in their bird life, particularly the summer migrants here to feed their young on the Oaks rich insect life. Llysdinam first put up nest boxes before the First World War and they have been present and in use ever since making it one of the oldest nest-boxed sites in existence.

The bird which uses these most is the Pied Flycatcher (right), a small black and white bird which commutes to and from Africa each autumn and spring often returning to the same woodland if not the same box to breed in successive years. Ringing these birds with a small lightweight ring on one leg has enabled scientist to track these birds on migration from Llysdinam, via Dorset to the French coast then along the Bay of Biscay and through Spain and Portugal before heading across Morocco for the winter. Their return here in early April and their egg-laying a month or so later has got earlier almost annually since the 1980s which could be evidence of global warming.

Other birds of these woods include Redstart, Wood and Willow Warblers, Nuthatch (right), Treecreeper, Blue, Great and Marsh tits (with Coal Tits and Goldcrests if there are a few conifers around). Larger birds of these woods include Raven, Buzzard and increasingly the Red Kite together with the ubiquitous pigeons and crow family.

57

One of the most renowned populations of toads is that at Llandrindod Lake made famous by over two decades of study by Llysdinam Field Centre. In many local ponds, frogs and toads live next to smooth, Palmate and great crested newts as they do in many places. At Llysdinam, however, a palmate/smooth newt hybrid

(pictured left) was collected from a pond there. A truly unique animal! The woods are home to most of the common small mammals such as voles, mice and shrews. Notably, the rarely seen water shrew falls into pitfall traps at the Llysdinam Field Centre and our usual "house mouse" is the Yellow-necked Mouse, a larger and generally more locally distributed relative of the common Field Mouse. Of the larger mammals, Badgers, Foxes, Rabbits are common, and the Hare is less frequently seen but still around. Stoats and Weasels are present but their larger relatives tend to hog the limelight for various reasons. The Polecat, once restricted to west and mid-Wales has now spread well into central England; the invading American Mink is ever present - and if you see a small very dark "otter" near the river which has little fear of humans - that will be a mink!

More intriguing is the status of a much rarer member of the same family, the Pine Marten (right). Although common in Scotland there are a scattering of records particularly along the mid-Wye of identifiable scats (droppings) but few reliable sightings. Of the even larger animals, a Muntjac

Deer was seenat Llysdinam a few years ago but not since, and Roe Deer are probably in the forestry plantations to the east.

Where are the best places to see wildlife around Newbridge? Try a walk along the footpath from the rear of the Vicarage along the river upstream to beach area - but not on a summer's day unless you want to visit the Costa del Newbridge! A walk around Aberithon Turbary at any time of year will always provide something worthwhile to watch and in autumn you may be lucky enough to see flocks of birds coming to roost in the reed bed there.

Connections with well known Naturalists

For its size, Newbridge has had a considerable amount of attention from eminent naturalists which no doubt reflects the richness of its superb countryside.

Sir David Attenborough has filmed at Cors y Llyn, David Bellamy at what is now BSW Timber, Gerald Durrell used the River Wye near here in one of his films; Eric Hosking, one of Britain's best ever nature photographers lost an eye to a Tawny Owl just north of the village – hence the title of his autobiography "An Eye for a Bird". The late Sir Michael Venables Llewelyn of Llysdinam helped found what is now the Radnorshire Wildlife Trust. His father Sir Charles was a knowledgeable naturalist and several of his forbearers were eminent in several biological disciplines.

Sir Charles Venables-Llewelyn

Gerald Durrell filming in the Wye near Newbridge – 1983

Photograph of Tawny Owl by Eric Hosking.

Walks around Newbridge

Around the village there are several signposted paths and bridleways which make pleasant walks. All are shown on 1:50,000 Ordnance Survey map sheet 147 as dotted or dashed red lines.

1.   Newbridge to Disserth. (Paths LNY 48,49 & 50)

Turn onto the signposted bridleway near the school entrance through Knaplands estate and on to Disserth. This track originally lead to the old Castlebach part of the ancient Woodcastle estate.

2.   Ridgemount, the Old Railway & Aberithon Turbary (LNY47)

From the village green, pass the church and then about 200 yards further on a bridleway is signposted to the right. This broad track was once used by the Drovers bringing their animals from west Wales to the markets of England. The bridleway heads towards the river but on reaching the old railway it turns sharply left. The path follows left along the old railway track and descends down the left hand side of the demolished bridge onto the Aberithon track. Turn left and either follow the track back to the road and the village or go through the first gate on the right (close it after you!) and walk around the Aberithon turbary — an ancient peat cutting site — which once provided fuel for the village and is now a nature reserve.

3.   Llyn Cam (LNY 51A)

Take the Beulah road towards the Wye Bridge, follow footpath sign to right past a row of cottages. This leads you down to the river and upstream as far as the foundations of the old railway bridge.

Snippets of history to find while you are walking:

1.   Pipe and Jug (alehouse) motif above cottage window (right)

2.   Timber from 18th Century bridge in river bed

3.   Preserved section of old Brynwern Bridge

4.   Stone on bridge naming James Watt as benefactor

5.   Jubilee stone

6.   Standing stone

7.   Rock well — original village water supply

Walks around Newbridge

For those who want to go further afield the uninhabited rolling tops of the Cambrian Mountains are within a few minutes drive of the village offering one of the largest unspoilt wilderness areas in England and Wales.

The Wye Valley Walk. On the west side of the river this signposted walk will take you from Rhayader via Newbridge to Builth and beyond.

Walk back from Llandrindod "the pretty way" by taking the lane on the left soon after crossing the Ithon bridge on the outskirts of Llandrindod. This eventually brings you back onto the B4358 about 1.5 miles from Newbridge.

Take the *A470 south* from Newbridge, cross Pont a'r Ithon and take the bridle way signposted to the left a couple of hundred yards further on and, using a map, follow one of the several rights of way which lead from it. The bridleway through to the A483(T) is probably the best.

The open hills to the west can be accessed at several points:-

Drive north towards Rhayader on the A470. Turn left over bridge into Llanwrthwl village. Follow the second turn left until it leads to open hill (For a scenic drive follow through Llanwrthwl village take the left hand turn to Elan Village possibly returning back down the right hand road).

Cross the Wye bridge in Newbridge, turn immediately right, straight across at the crossroads and follow track onto hill (Do not park beyond the crossroads).

Head out of Newbridge on the Beulah road. After about 3 miles there is a post box on a house on the right hand side of the road. Turn right and follow this road for about 2.5 miles from where the tracks lead to Llanwrthwl and the Elan Valley.